Pebble™ Plus

A Visit to

The Airport

by Patricia J. Murphy

Consulting Editor: Gail Saunders-Smith, PhD
Reading Consultant: Jennifer Norford, Senior Consultant
Mid-continent Research for Education and Learning
Aurora, Colorado

Capstone press

Mankato, Minnesota

Pebble Plus is published by Capstone Press
151 Good Counsel Drive, P.O. Box 669, Mankato, Minnesota 56002
www.capstonepress.com

1 2 3 4 5 6 09 08 07 06 05 04

Library of Congress Cataloging-in-Publication Data
Murphy, Patricia J., 1963–
    The airport/by Patricia J. Murphy.
    p. cm.—(Pebble plus: A visit to)
    Includes bibliographical references and index.
    ISBN 0-7368-2578-9 (hardcover)
    1. Airports—Juvenile literature. [1. Airports.] I. Title. II. Series: Pebble Plus, a visit to (Mankato, Minn.)
TL725.15.M87 2005
387.7′36—dc22
                         2003024948

Summary: Simple text and photographs present a visit to the airport.

Editorial Credits
Sarah L. Schuette, editor; Enoch Peterson, book designer; Jennifer Bergstrom, series designer;
    Wanda Winch, photo researcher; Karen Hieb, product planning editor

Photo Credits
Capstone Press/Gary Sundermeyer, cover (pilot), 6–7, 11, 12–13, 16–17, 21
Corbis/George Shelley, 4–5; Royalty-Free, 9
Corel, back cover
Folio Inc./Rob Crandall, cover (control tower)
Jorge Miguel Abreu, 14–15
Konstantin von Wedelstaedt, cover (airplane)
PhotoDisc/Jack Hollingsworth, 18–19
Transportation Security Administration, 1

Capstone Press thanks the Mankato Regional Airport in Mankato, Minnesota, for photo shoot assistance.

Note to Parents and Teachers

The series A Visit to supports national social studies standards related to the production, distribution, and consumption of goods and services. This book describes and illustrates a visit to an airport. The images support early readers in understanding the text. The repetition of words and phrases helps early readers learn new words. This book also introduces early readers to subject-specific vocabulary words, which are defined in the Glossary section. Early readers may need assistance to read some words and to use the Table of Contents, Glossary, Read More, Internet Sites, and Index/Word List sections of the book.

Word Count: 105
Early-Intervention Level: 12

Table of Contents

The Airport

People use the airport every day. They take trips and go on vacations.

Travelers stand in line
at ticket counters.
They show their tickets
and check their bags.

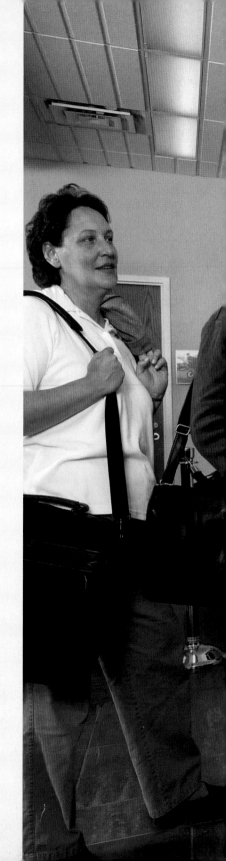

Travelers go through security
at the terminal. Security
workers keep airplanes safe.

Travelers wait for airplanes
to take off and land.

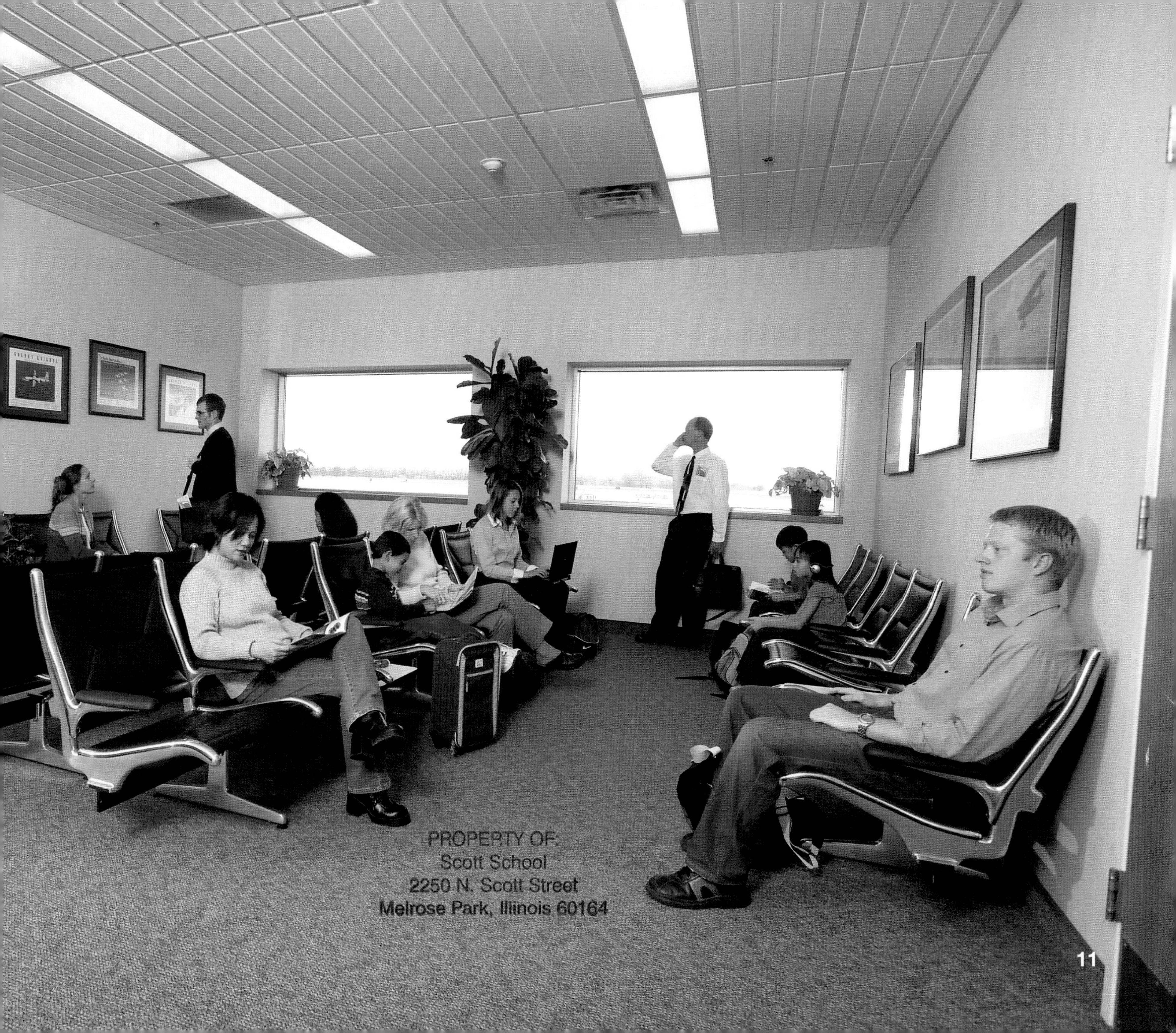

Around the Airport

Airport workers get
airplanes ready.
They check, fix, and
clean airplanes.

13

Flight control workers work
in towers. They tell pilots
where to go.

Taking Off

Airplanes take off and land
on runways. Workers direct
airplanes on runways
with lights.

Flight attendants
show passengers how
to be safe on flights.

Pilots fly airplanes to many places around the world.

Glossary

flight attendant—a person who helps passengers and serves food and beverages on an airplane

flight control worker—a person who helps guide an airplane; flight control workers give pilots directions and other information.

pilot—a person who flies an airplane; pilots sit in cockpits.

security worker—a person who checks to make sure nothing unsafe gets on airplanes; security workers check travelers' bags and clothing.

terminal—a section of an airport

Read More

Gish, Melissa. *An Airport.* Field Trips. North Mankato, Minn.: Smart Apple Media, 2003.

Hill, Mary. *Signs at the Airport.* Signs in My World. New York: Children's Press, 2003.

Radabaugh, Melinda Beth. *Going on an Airplane.* First Time. Chicago: Heinemann Library, 2003.

Internet Sites

FactHound offers a safe, fun way to find Internet sites related to this book. All of the sites on FactHound have been researched by our staff.

Here's how:

1. Visit *www.facthound.com*

2. Type in this special code **0736825789** for age-appropriate sites. Or enter a search word related to this book for a more general search.

3. Click on the **Fetch It** button.

FactHound will fetch the best sites for you!

Index/Word List